ABOUT ANIMALS

ABOUT ANIMALS

with illustrations by
Richard Scarry

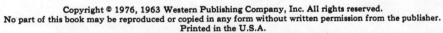

gb Golden Press • New York

Western Publishing Company, Inc.
Racine, Wisconsin

Farm Animals

Many animals live on this farm. The pig lives in the pigsty. The cow lives in the pasture.

Do you see a sheep eating grass? Can you find the baby sheep? We call a baby sheep a lamb.

Horses like to eat grass, too, but this horse has found something even better. Can you see what it is?

Here is a family of chickens. The father is called a rooster. The mother is a hen. And the baby is called a chick. Can you point to each one?

Zoo Animals

The mouse school has come to the zoo to look at all the animals. Let's see what animals they have found.

Two mice are looking at a deer with long horns. Two are watching a lion with a bushy mane. Two mice are looking at a striped tiger and two more are looking at a spotted leopard.

How many mice are looking at the buffalo and the camel?

Can you tell the names of all the animals in the zoo?

Look! Here are more zoo animals. There
is an elephant mother and her baby. Did you
know that a baby elephant is called a calf?
What other baby animal is called a calf?

There are two more big animals in cages.
Can you point to the bear and the gorilla?

Here is the zookeeper. She feeds and takes care of all the animals. Right now it is the seal's dinnertime. What does the seal like to eat?

Now you have seen the animals in the zoo. Which is your favorite animal?

Birds

barn swallow

sparrow

wren

robin

starling

tern

seagull

owl

nest

baby robins

pheasant

ground dove

quail

woodcock

crow

puffin

goose

sandpiper

canary

bittern

duck

duckling

stork

swan

pigeon

What a lot of birds! They all have feathers, two wings, two legs, and a tail, but how different they look!

Point to a bird with a forked tail. Can you find the swan, owl, pigeon, and goose?

Can you find some blue eggs in a nest? How many are there?

Strange and Beautiful Birds

penguin

spoonbill

cardinal

pelican

ostrich

baby ostrich

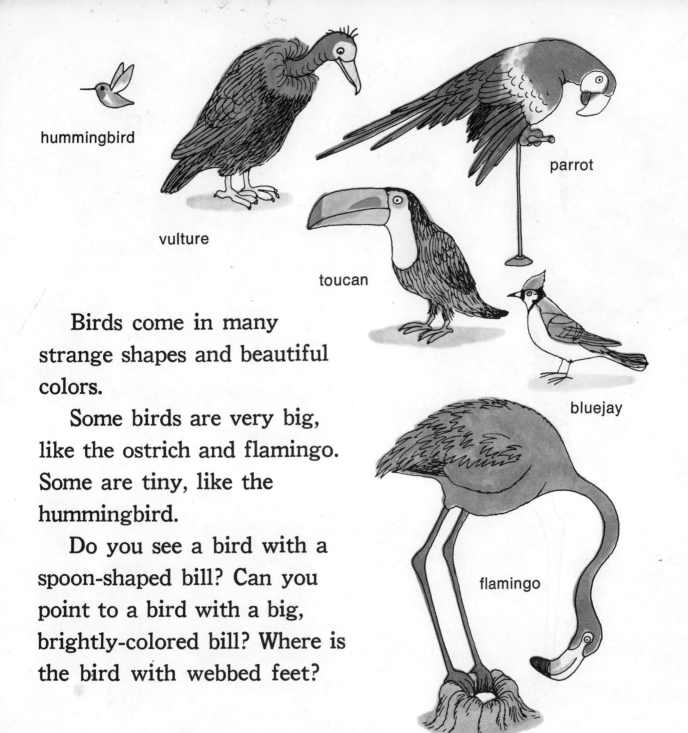

hummingbird

vulture

toucan

parrot

bluejay

flamingo

Birds come in many strange shapes and beautiful colors.

Some birds are very big, like the ostrich and flamingo. Some are tiny, like the hummingbird.

Do you see a bird with a spoon-shaped bill? Can you point to a bird with a big, brightly-colored bill? Where is the bird with webbed feet?

worm

ladybugs

butterfly

ants

caterpillar

mosquito

more caterpillars

moth

firefly

cricket

beetle

fly

hermit crab

sea horse

bee

dragonfly

Large and Small Animals

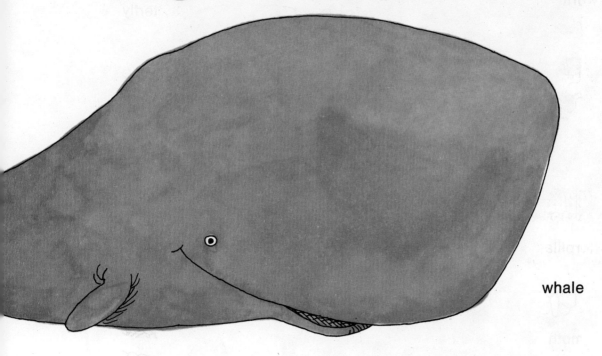

whale

    Here is a very large animal. It is the largest animal in the world. Do you know what it is called? It is called a whale, and it lives in the ocean.

    There are many small animals in this picture, too. Which of them have you seen in your yard? Some of these animals crawl, some fly, some jump. Do any of them swim?

Circus Animals

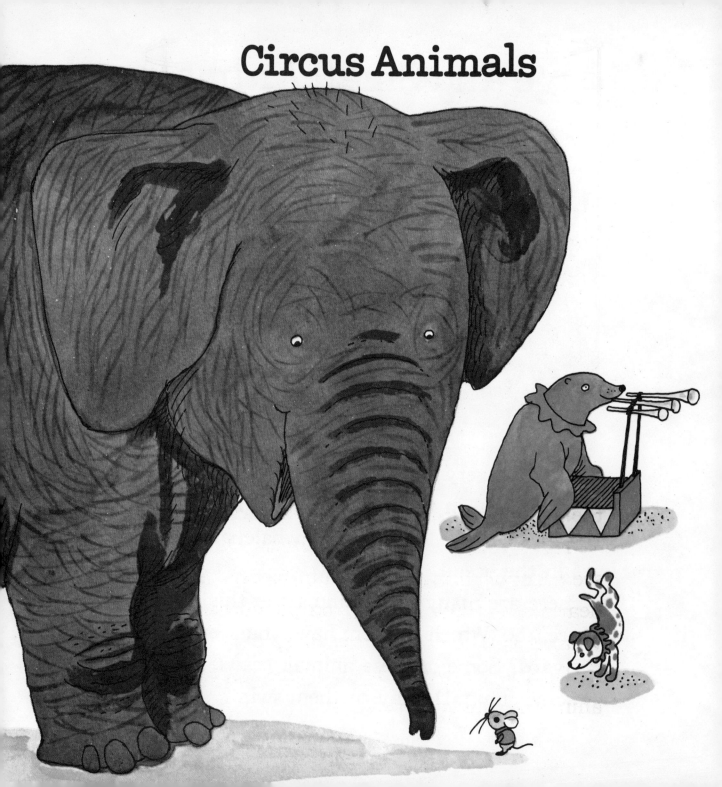

The lion tamer is trying to teach the lion a new trick. He wants the lion to jump through the hoop. Do you think the lion will do it?

Have you ever been to a circus? Did you see a dog walking on its front paws? Did you hear a seal playing a tune on the horns? What is your favorite circus animal?

Do you know the name of the biggest animal in this picture?

alligator—in a swamp

frog—in a pond

reindeer—in the cold North

walrus—in icy waters

tiger—in the jungle
(where do you suppose he found that boot?)

leopard—in the jungle

penguin—in lands of
ice and snow

Wild Animals

Most wild animals do not live in the
zoo or at the circus. They live free, in
many different kinds of places. Do you
know the names of these animals and
where each of them lives?

zebra—on the plains
of Africa

kangaroo and baby—on the
plains of Australia

Sea Animals

Many sea animals live in shells they make themselves. Can you point to some? Did you know that the hermit crab cannot make its own shell? It finds a leftover shell from some other sea animal to live in.

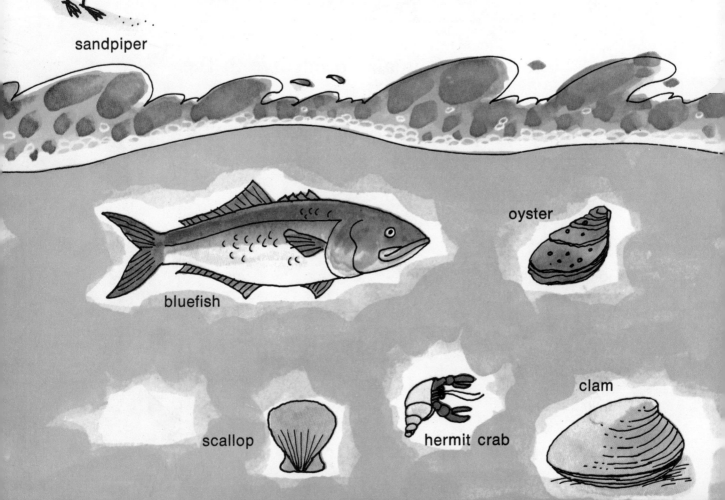

sandpiper

bluefish

oyster

scallop

hermit crab

clam

Only one animal in the picture does not live in the sea. It is the sandpiper, a bird that finds its food on the beaches.

Point to:

crab	starfish	seaweed
clam	hermit crab	oyster
fish	sandpiper	shrimp

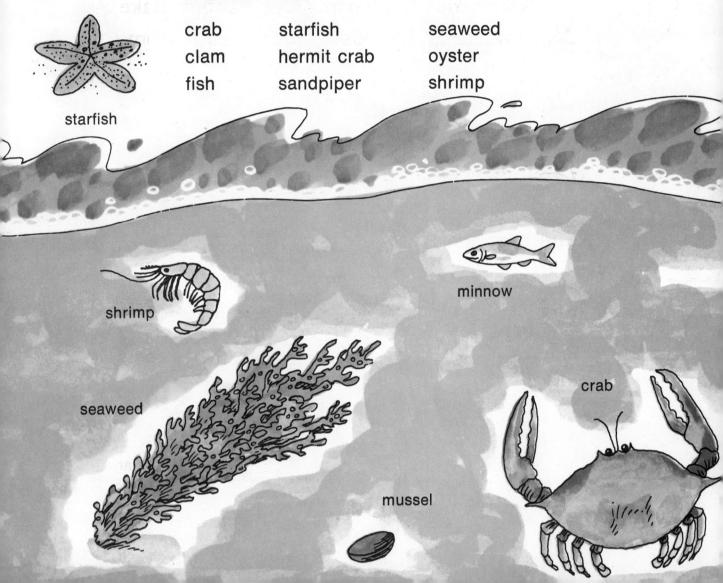

starfish

shrimp

minnow

seaweed

crab

mussel

Fat and Thin

Here are two animals.
One is fat and one is thin.

What is the name of the
fat one? He is a pig.

Do you know what that
very thin bird is called? That
very thin bird is a stork.

Can you think of some
other fat and thin animals?
Is a snake fat or thin? Is an
elephant fat or thin?

Tall and Short

Here are two more animals. One is very tall and the other is very short. What is the name of the tall one? What is the name of the short one?

The tall one is a giraffe. The giraffe eats the leaves at the tops of trees. He needs his long legs and long neck to reach his dinner.

The turtle has very short legs. Luckily, he does not have to walk far, for he always carries his house with him on his back.

THE
END